Long Ago In Be

An Advent course for small g ...ps on the Book of Ruth

Amy Scott Robinson

kevin mayhew

First Published in 2024 by Kevin Mayhew Ltd,

Fengate Farm,

Rattlesden,

Bury St Edmunds,

Suffolk, IP30 0SZ

Copyright © 2024 Amy Scott Robinson

ISBN (paperback): 9781838582135

ISBN (eBook): 9781838582142

Paperback product code: 1501744

eBook product code: 1501745

All rights reserved.

No part of this book may be reproduced in any form or by any electronic or mechanical means, including information storage and retrieval systems, without written permission from the author, except for the use of brief quotations in a book review.

All Bible quotations are taken from the NRSV(A)

For my sister, who chose the name Ruth and lives up to it.

Contents

Introduction

The book of Ruth is a little jewel of the Old Testament: a tale of two widows, with themes of loyalty, love and hope. Although the genealogy at the end shows that the story is being told to an audience after the time of King David, the first sentence of the book shows that the action takes place much earlier, 'in the days when the judges ruled'.

Judges must be one of the most uncomfortable books of the Bible: it spans generations as it spirals into destruction, finishing in a lawless time of horrific inhumanity, and God having seemingly abandoned his people to their all-consuming sin. In contrast, Ruth is a gentle story about the personal lives and decisions of two women and the kindness they show to each other, and are shown by others.

Beautifully, it is through this very domestic story, and not through the big-picture battling of tribes and leaders going on at the same time, that we see God working out his salvation plan: Ruth's family is the family of Jesus, her loyal choices leading her directly to become part of the ancestry of Christ. The book of Ruth shows us that whatever wars and terrors are going on in our broken world, God continues to work in the ordinary lives of faithful individuals and families.

In fact, reading the book of Ruth as we near Christmas time, we hear the resonances of another small family, another faithful and loyal young woman, another new baby, and another story that all took place in the same city - long ago in Bethlehem.

How to use this book

This book has been written for people meeting weekly in a small group setting over Advent, so for some of the activities, I am addressing a group leader when I suggest ways to approach them. However, this resource can be used in many other ways.

Each session has an introduction to the passage, an opening question or activity, readings, and a reflection. The sessions also have suggestions for prayer activities, songs and journaling prompts. None of these are obligatory! You could keep it really simple by combining the introduction and reflection for each week into a short talk and simply using the opening prayer, readings, talk and closing prayer. In this way, the material could be woven into a regular service such as morning or evening prayer, or form the basis of a short act of worship for a group that meets socially, before or after their other usual activities.

Most of the sessions include both a group activity and a prayer activity which involve a certain amount of preparation and moving about. One way to simplify a session would be to choose only one of these to do thoroughly, replacing the other with a short time of quiet journaling or by saying a short prayer together, depending on the preferences of your group.

Alternatively, you could use all the material the book has to offer, add some ideas of your own, and ask other people to join in as musicians, readers, artists and refreshment providers to run a weekly event which could be offered to the community.

You could select material and run all the sessions together as a single Advent event instead of running them weekly. You could use the reflections and readings in your regular Sunday services. You could also read the book as an individual, using the reflections, discussion questions and journaling prompts as suggestions for your own Advent quiet times, and going through the material at your own pace.

However you use this book, I pray that you have a peaceful and blessed Advent reading about the two Bethlehem stories and how they fit into God's great plan of salvation.

Prepare

At the end of every session, there is a 'prepare' section aimed mainly at the group leader, with a summary of what is needed for the next session. This is to give a quick overview and an indication of how much time might need to be spent gathering resources; more details can be found in the relevant sections of the sessions themselves.

For the first session, you may wish to use a map of the ancient Jordan Valley and find the places mentioned in the readings ahead of time. Depending on your group, you might want to ask them all to bring journals or notebooks and something to write with ahead of time; otherwise, have a look at the group activity to decide what to provide in terms of paper or print-outs. For the prayer activity, there are two options: you will want to choose one and have a look at the resources needed for it as you prepare.

Throughout the course, there are words and images to be displayed where everyone can see them. A PowerPoint presentation and a screen would be very useful; failing that, you might want to get hold of a flipchart. Otherwise, you could provide individual print-outs, in which case you might want to put aside time to look through the sessions and prepare all of them as a booklet ahead of the course.

Chapter 1

Session One

Beginning the Journey

BEGIN

Introduction

Both the Christmas story and the book of Ruth begin with a journey to Bethlehem. Although the journeys are taken for very different reasons, both of them could be called a reluctant homecoming. For Naomi, the journey back to her home town represents loss and failure. Her time spent in Moab, trying to escape a famine with her family, has ended with the death of her husband and both her sons. Her only option now is to return to Bethlehem in the hope that somebody - perhaps a distant relation - might remember her and take pity on her. As a widow, past the age of having more children, she will need to rely on others for the rest of her life.

For Joseph and Mary, the journey is made reluctantly because it has been imposed on them by an oppressive regime that has suddenly decided to count and categorise everybody in the world - or at least, in the Roman empire. Joseph has to take

Mary to his home town of Bethlehem, despite the fact that she is pregnant. She will have to leave her mother and all the women who would have helped her to give birth, leave her familiar home and belongings, and make the uncomfortable journey. Like Naomi, Mary and Joseph may have been wondering who would be there to greet them - some of Joseph's relatives, perhaps, who hadn't seen him since he was small? In a crowded city at a time of upheaval, they could be relying on these near-strangers for food, shelter and safety.

As we begin the journey through Advent towards Christmas, we join these people making two different journeys to Bethlehem in their apprehension, sadness, hopes and fears. We are leaving the old year behind us, with all its joyful moments and devastating losses, and heading into a new one. It may not be a joyful setting out, and it may not feel convenient with everything that has to be done at this time of year - but we have travelling companions, and we know that our eventual destination is back home, where our roots are.

Opening question/activity

What was the worst journey you have ever been on?

And what was the best? Think only about the journey - not the destination, event or holiday after you arrived!

Tell the story!

* * *

WORSHIP

Pray

Heavenly Father, as we gather, meet us in the little journeys of our days - those of us who are busy, who are tired, who are worrying about the last thing, who are looking forward to the next thing. Help us to take this time to rest and focus on you. Meet us in the big journeys of our lives - those of us who are just starting out, those who don't know where they are going, those who are facing mountain climbs or standing on mountain tops, those of us in the valley of shadows. Help us to come together in support of each other and in the knowledge of your love for each of us.

Meet us on the journey of this Advent course. May we learn more about you, your word and your salvation story. May it speak to us, change us, comfort us and sustain us as we travel. Amen.

Sing

Here are some suggestions for hymns and songs which you could sing or listen to as you worship together:

The journey of life by Valerie Collison
One more step by Sydney Carter
To be a pilgrim by Percy Dearmer
Father, hear the prayer we offer by Love M. Whitcomb Willis

Read

Bible passages: Ruth 1:1-14, Luke 2:1-5

Ideas to support the readings

Look online to find a map of the ancient Jordan Valley, and mark the places named in the readings. Judah (or Judea in some translations) is the region where Jerusalem and Bethlehem are found. Bethlehem and Moab are on opposite sides of the Dead Sea, whereas Galilee is a region further north. You could use a printout or basic drawing of the map to mark the places as they are named in the readings.

* * *

EXPLORE

Reflection

Naomi thinks that this is the end of her story. Her words to her two daughters-in-law show her complete loss of all hope. Not only has she lost her husband, but both her sons have died, and they were her only links to these two young Moabite women. Ruth and Orpah have nothing else to share with Naomi - no grandchildren, no common culture, they don't even worship the same gods. There is no reason for the three women to stay together.

The best option for the two young ones is to find new husbands. Widows in that culture had no way of making a life for themselves; they relied on the charity of their community until they once again had a man to provide for them, and when they were older, they relied on their sons or sons-in-law. But Naomi is too old to get married again, and as she points out to Ruth and Orpah, even if she did remarry she is too old to have more children, and even if that were possible, they wouldn't arrive fully grown to be available as husbands! Naomi cannot think of a single thing she has going for her. This journey is the end.

Mary knows that this is the beginning of her story. She has already made her journey to Elizabeth's house (which we will look at in the next session) and she remembers what the angel Gabriel said. This journey may be unexpected, and the future may be largely unknown, but Mary knows that the child in her womb is the Son of God - Gabriel said so. She is carrying hope, not just for herself, but for her people and for the world. She begins her journey filled with endless possibilities.

So Mary knows that she is at the beginning, and Naomi is sure that she has reached the end. However, despite her belief that all is lost, Naomi would not be making the journey at all if she did not have the tiniest flicker of hope. She has heard that the famine in Judah is over: there is a rumour in Moab that the Lord has 'had consideration for his people and given them food' (verse 6). After more than a decade of living in a foreign land, there is just a little chance that there might be something for her back home.

Sometimes, hope can be so small that it is barely discernible; but we cannot survive without it. If Naomi had not heard that rumour, she might have just stayed in Moab and died, without a chance that the community in this place where she was a refugee would support her. I wonder whether the rumour rekindled a little bit of faith in her, too? It's not just that there is food in Judah, but that the Lord has considered his people. Even though Naomi believes that the hand of the Lord has turned against her (verse 14) there is still a note of the possibility that God might be faithful, that he has remembered his people after all. Even though it is still faint and in the background, it is enough for Naomi to start the return journey - and her first steps are the catalyst for the rest of the story.

Discussion

- Where is 'home' for you?
- If you had to go on a long journey, travelling by foot, what would you take with you - and what would have to be left behind?
- Who would be your ideal travelling companion?
- Think about the four people we have met in the readings: Naomi and Ruth, Joseph and Mary. What thoughts and emotions might they each be experiencing as they set out? Which one resonates most with you?
- What do you hope for? Can you think of a time when you nearly lost hope? What kept you going?

Group activity

In this activity, the group will 'pack a bag' for the journey of Advent. You could provide paper with the outline of a suitcase printed on it, or you could invite people to make their own notes, in the form of words or pictures, in their own journals. If they do so, you could invite them to begin by drawing the outline of a suitcase or bag in the middle of the page, but leaving space around the outside. Then read the following, leaving space between the paragraphs for everyone to respond on their paper:

We are going to pack our bags for the journey of Advent, the journey towards Christmas and through this course.

First, let's consider what we are leaving behind. Use the area outside the shape of your bag to write or draw anything you don't want with you - perhaps an attitude, a habit or a stress that you will try to put down and leave behind this Advent. Perhaps it's a memory that often haunts you at this time of year, and you would like to ask for God's help to leave it behind this time.

Naomi's journey started with loss. Also outside the bag, we can write or draw the people or things that we are sad to leave behind us this year, but we have to, because we don't have them with us any more. Draw them in a separate area of the page to the others if you like, to acknowledge that these are painful losses, things we wish we could have back and take with us.

Now, inside the bag, we will write or draw the things we would like to take with us in this season of Advent, things we might need for the journey. We might be wanting to pray more, learn more, have some peaceful moments or even just the occasional opportunity to breathe, as this season can be so chaotic!

Lastly, write in a little corner of the bag a hope that you have for this season, for what Christmas might be like or might mean to you this year. Even if it's just the slightest glimmer of hope, even if it seems far-fetched, we will carry it with us.

* * *

RESPOND

Pray

There are two themes to pick up from today's passages: a theme of journeying, exile, refuge and home; and a theme of loss, grief and hope. Here are some prayers and suggestions for each of them.

First theme: Prayer for refugees. You could make a visual display using any recent news about refugees, or search for images and artwork online. *The Travellers*, a series of sculptures by Bruno Catalano also known as *Les Voyageurs*, would make a good focus. Pictures could be laid out on the floor or a table, or a PowerPoint could show them while music plays. Invite people to consider the images and respond quietly in their own way before joining together in this closing prayer.
Lord, we ask your blessing and protection for all those who have had to leave their homes because of war, famine, disaster or threat. We pray for them as they travel, seeking a place of safety. May you bring them comfort and hope. We ask, too, that you guide and equip all those who work to provide shelter and safety for refugees all over the world; and that your hand is on all the places they flee from, that you are bringing peace and safety so that one day those places become welcome homelands once again. Amen.

Second theme: A remembrance of loved ones. You could have a tree to hang names from, or a place to light a candle quietly; if possible, arrange it so that these can stay and be revisited through Advent.
Lord, we pray for all those who are grieving. Christmas can make it even harder to miss someone. We thank you that you

are God With Us, who came to earth, experienced your own grief and comforted your friends in theirs. We pray that you would draw near to everyone experiencing grief and loss in this season, bringing your comfort, peace and promise of everlasting life. Show us how to hope and trust in your promises, and rest in your love for us. Amen.

Ponder

A question to think about for next time:
If you could give some advice to Naomi, Ruth, Joseph or Mary at this point in their story, which one would you speak to and what would you say?

Prepare

For group leaders: Next time, we will be looking at Ruth 1:15-22 and Luke 1:39-56. You might want to read the passages ahead of the session.

For these readings, you may want to follow the suggestion given in the next section and dramatise them, using two women to read the parts of Naomi/Elizabeth and Ruth/Mary. In that case, choose those two readers now so that they can prepare their parts, and make sure that they will be able to be there for the session. You may want to print off the readings (eg from Bible Gateway online) and highlight the parts for the readers in advance.

For the group activity next time, you may want to see if anyone in the group is good at lettering or has artistic leanings to help you prepare. You will need a way to display some words, as beautifully as possible, where everyone can see them.

For group members: If you have not started a journal, now

would be a good time to do so, as there will be a chance to use it in the next few sessions! Find a notebook that you can doodle in - plain paper is best - and spend some time before the next session to make notes of everything that has interested you so far. You could illustrate some of the story or create a messy mind map of your thoughts. You could also note down your answer to the question under 'Ponder'.

Chapter 2

Session Two

Bitter and Blessed

BEGIN

Introduction

What's in a name? Do you know the meaning of your own name, or which language it comes from? It may seem strange to give a child a name with an unpleasant or sad meaning, but in scripture, it seems to happen fairly frequently, especially among the prophets who are told to name their children things like 'No Mercy' and 'Not My People' as a sign and reminder of God's warning (Hosea 1:6-8). A popular name for girls in the Hebrew language was Mary (or Mara, Maryam, Miriam). It means 'bitter'. Perhaps the frequency of oppression led to the popularity of this name: Miriam, the sister of Moses, for example, was born into slavery in Egypt; Mary, the mother of Jesus was born into Roman occupation.

Naomi, on the other hand, means 'pleasant'; yet when Naomi arrives in Bethlehem in today's reading, and is greeted by her name, she responds 'Call me no longer Naomi, call me Mara, for the Almighty has dealt bitterly with me' (Ruth 1:20).

In the NRSV, this passage is set out in verse: Naomi is pouring out a song or psalm of lament. In contrast, when Mary visits her cousin Elizabeth in today's passage from Luke, she sings the words we now know as the Magnificat: a song of praise, gratitude and worship to the God who has looked on her with favour. 'From now on,' she says, 'all generations will call me blessed' (Luke 1:48).

The woman whose name means pleasant says 'Call me bitter'. The woman whose name means bitter sings 'Call me blessed'.

Many things are spoken over us as we grow. Our names, our circumstances and our backgrounds may cause others to think that they can predict what our lives will look like. But both Mary and Naomi, in their stories, will discover a faithful God who can turn things around, so that eventually both women will be called 'blessed'; and we can share their blessing.

In this session we will take a deeper look at Naomi's lament and Mary's song of praise, and at a third song as well: the beautiful piece of verse spoken to Naomi by her faithful daughter-in-law, whose name, Ruth, means 'friend'.

Opening question/activity

Listen to feedback for the question that ended the last session: if you could give some advice to Naomi, Ruth, Joseph or Mary at this point in their story, which one would you speak to and what would you say?

What does your name mean? If you could choose a name for

yourself at this point in your life, what would you want its meaning to be?

* * *

WORSHIP

Pray

Lord, as we come to read the heart songs of these three women, we bring you the secret songs of our own hearts. We call to mind our longings, our griefs, our hopes and our passions. We pour them all out to you.
(Leave some silence here, or perhaps play a short piece of music, for people to consider these things.)
May the study of your word touch our lives today, adding your praise and glory to the songs of our hearts.
Amen.

Sing

Here are some suggestions for hymns and songs which you could sing or listen to as you worship together:

Tell Out My Soul by Timothy Dudley-Smith (this hymn uses Mary's words from the Magnificat)
O Jesus, I have promised by John Ernest Bode
Brother, sister, let me serve you by Richard Gillard
There are also musical settings of Ruth's song and the Magnificat to be found on YouTube, Spotify etc.

Read

Bible passages: Ruth 1:15-22 and Luke 1:39-56

Ideas to support the readings
Choose two women (if possible, one younger and one older) and a narrator to read these readings. Have the same woman read both Naomi and Elizabeth's parts, and the other read both Ruth and Mary. They should read whenever there is direct speech for those characters. It will then be possible to hear clearly how each woman has a heart song in each reading.

* * *

EXPLORE

Reflection
These passages, in both stories, are rather like the moment in a musical when every character gets one verse of a song to express what is on their mind in that moment. The four women, Ruth, Naomi, Elizabeth and Mary each have a moment of pouring out their hearts, and although each song comes from a different mood and background, they blend together in the moment of the story. What is each woman singing about?

Ruth (Ruth 1:16-17) has a song of insistent, compassionate faithfulness. Even the structure of her words, with a word repeated in every line, gives the impression of two people shoulder to shoulder together. She vows to take on everything that is Naomi's, thus leaving her own ties behind: she says that Naomi's land, people, and even God will now be hers. It is no wonder that this is a popular reading at weddings. Ruth's promise is complete, and she will not take no for an answer. She reassures Naomi that nothing will change her mind, until Naomi sees that Ruth is 'determined to go with her' and accepts her offer of love and companionship. Ruth's song, although it comes from a human heart, carries echoes of Old Testament descriptions of God's faithfulness to his people, such as the repeated promise in Deuteronomy 31:6-8: 'It is the Lord who goes with you; he will not fail you or forsake you.'

Naomi's (Ruth 1:20-21) is a song of lament, in which she declares herself to be 'bitter' and 'empty'. She pours out her grief and loss: 'I went away full, but the Lord has brought me back empty'. She insists that she can no longer live up to her name, which means 'pleasant', and should instead be called Mara, meaning bitter. Saying this as she returns to her homeland shows the disconnection she feels from the person she was when she last lived there. She has lost everything since then. She is trying to express to her old friends that she is simply not the same person any more, not the Naomi they knew and have recognised. In her bitterness, she rebuffs their welcome and recognition, and she ignores the promises of her faithful daughter-in-law; she refuses to see any of the hope that God is putting in front of her, instead saying that God has 'dealt harshly' with her and 'brought calamity' on her. She is too deep in her grief to see the way forward, or the help that is already being offered to her.

Fast forward more than a thousand years, and elderly Elizabeth feels her unborn miracle child leaping in her womb as she greets Mary. The text (Luke 1:41) says that she was filled with the Holy Spirit, and the words she says also have a poetic structure, with two 'blessed' statements, then two observations, then another 'blessed'. Although she is calling Mary 'blessed', her statements show how blessed she feels herself: 'And why has this happened to me, that the mother of my Lord comes to me?' (verse 43). Her final 'blessed' could refer to both women: 'Blessed is she who believed that there would be a fulfilment of what was spoken to her by the Lord' (verse 45). Both Mary and Elizabeth have waited for a fulfilment of a promise given to them by an angel, and the children they are both carrying are the ones they were promised. So, tucked away in the centre of her song is Elizabeth's unborn baby leaping for joy, encapsulating this moment of being sure that God has kept his promises.

Finally and most famously, Mary sings the Magnificat. It comes as an answer to Elizabeth's song, picking up on the older woman's greeting of 'blessed are you among women' to say 'all generations will call me blessed' (verse 48). Mary follows Elizabeth's statement of promises fulfilled to list the many promises that will be fulfilled in Jesus: scattering the proud, bringing down the powerful, filling the hungry, all 'according to the promise he made to our ancestors' (verse 55). Her words are prophetic: they will be echoed by her son Jesus in his teachings. In Luke 6:26, Jesus lists blessings and woes which mention the hungry being filled and the full being hungry; the poor inheriting the kingdom, and the rich being woeful. Like Mary and Elizabeth, his list repeats the word 'blessed'.

So Mary and Elizabeth are united, inspired by the Holy Spirit to sing about the same things: their meeting brings their separate lives and experiences together into one moment of praise and wonder. Ruth and Naomi are still separated by Naomi's fog of grief and Ruth's inexperience of this new God, land and culture. Their moment of joy is yet to come. Yet their heart songs, even Naomi's bitter lament, are still heard by a loving God who knows his plans for them.

Discussion

- Which song resonates most with you? Why do you think that is?
- Do you think people tend to pray more when they are happy or sad? How about you?
- In Ruth 1:21, the phrase translated 'the LORD has dealt harshly with me' literally means 'The LORD has spoken against me'. It has the sense of being testified against in a court. Why do you think Naomi feels that way? Is she right to say that God is against her?
- In the Magnificat, Mary sings about all God's promises in the past tense, as if the hungry are already filled and the powerful are already brought down. Why do you think that is? How do you feel when you read those words?
- In a moment of overwhelming emotion, what helps you most - do you prefer to talk, keep it all in, journal, or turn to art or music? How could those preferences translate into ways of bringing your emotions to God?

Group activity

Create a way to feature a collection of words for all the group to see. In a large group, these could be printed together on individual sheets; in a smaller group, people could gather around a flipchart, large canvas or the words printed individually and laid out on the floor.

Use the following words in your collection:

Faithful, loyal, trusting, determined, empty, lost, lamenting, grieving, comforted, lifted, joyful, blessed, filled, fulfilled, favoured.

Shuffle them around in your display, perhaps creating a word cloud or representing them artistically if you can - you may be able to draw on the skills of a member in your group in advance. While playing some quiet, wordless background music, invite the group to consider the words prayerfully. Do any stand out? Do any seem to describe you? Offer those to God as your heart song. Do you wish any of them described you? Hold those up to God with longing, asking him to call you by those names. Leave time for people to write their words into their journals, or on paper, along with their prayers.

* * *

RESPOND

Pray

Allow the prayer time to blend into the end of the group activity, by asking everyone to gather back together and hold what they have drawn and written before God, as you say this prayer:

Father, you know the deepest longings of all our hearts, just as you did for Ruth, Naomi, Mary and Elizabeth. You know the plans you have for us, just as you did for them. Help us to trust you and to keep following you; guide us along our life's path. Amen.

Ponder

Everyone we meet has a unique story, with their own longings, griefs, regrets and joys that we cannot see, but God can. In the time between the sessions, try to be intentional about asking God to guide your conversations and encounters with the people you come across in the course of a day, and see whether it makes a difference to the way you approach your everyday meetings and tasks.

Prepare

For group leaders: do read over the next session carefully, as there is quite a lot of preparation and you may want to pick and choose!

You might like to find a way to show some illustrations during the readings: a PowerPoint would be the best way to do this. The activity will need some little figures or pebbles, one for each group member, and a 'shelter' which could be a box, table, the stable from a nativity scene or a cut-out in the shape of wings.

The prayer activity takes some local research, and you may want to assign some of this to the group members and ask everyone to bring something representing their chosen area to set the activity up together. You will also need a map of the local area and some post-it notes.

For group members: you might want to read ahead, as the reading from Ruth in the next session is quite long. There may also be an opportunity to talk about organisations that exist for marginalised people in your community. If you have any involvement with one of these, now would be a good moment to mention it to the group leader! You may want to gather some information to bring and share.

Chapter 3

Session Three

Long Lost Strangers

BEGIN

Introduction

We pick up the story of Ruth after the two women, Ruth and Naomi, have arrived in Bethlehem. At the beginning of chapter 2, we are told that Naomi has a distant relation there, or rather her late husband Elimelech does: his name is Boaz, and all we know so far is that he is from Elimelech's family. Although the writer of the Book of Ruth sets this information up at the beginning of the chapter, it appears to be quite by chance that Ruth finds herself in Boaz's field (verse 3). She has gone looking for a field in which to glean: in other words, picking up any grain that is left by the harvesters, as the poor and destitute were allowed to do according to God's law (Leviticus 23:22). As we shall see, Boaz will discover who Ruth is long before Ruth knows that there is any connection between them.

In the Christmas story, Mary and Joseph arrive in Bethlehem to find the place full because of the census. Although many Bible translations have given us the tradition that they stayed in a stable because an inn was full, it is more likely that the house of Joseph's distant relatives was full, since the whole family had to travel back to their hometown.

The word translated 'inn' can mean 'guest room'. With the house bursting at the seams, the family would have given Mary and Joseph the downstairs space, where the animals were kept. Even if they were Joseph's distant relations, they would never have met Mary, nor have had any idea of the significance of the child she was carrying.

So both Ruth and Mary are at the mercy of strangers, but strangers who have distant family connections to Naomi and to Joseph. Neither of them hope to receive anything but the very least of what might be expected: the leftover gleanings of grain, the outside area of a home. We will see how God meets both women on the very edge of these families, and begins his work of inclusion and support.

Opening question/activity

There is a well-known theory that everybody is just six degrees of separation - six social connections - away from each other. Send everyone around the room on a mission to find a connection to somebody famous, by asking others which famous people they, and people they know, have met. Any statement with fewer than six connections (eg 'My friend's brother's wife once met...') counts! Compare notes to see which was the smallest number of connections to the most well-known celebrity.

(People often have fun and interesting stories on this topic about people they have unlikely connections with, so you could also use some of this time to share those stories.)

* * *

WORSHIP

Pray

We bow our knees before the Father, from whom every family in heaven and on earth takes its name. (Ephesians 3:14-15)

Father, you have brought your people together here, and only you know all of our lives, all of our pasts, all of our possible connections. Nurture your family as we learn about you together: make us more like brothers and sisters to each other, and equip us to grow your church and welcome others in. Amen.

Sing

Here are some suggestions for hymns and songs which you could sing or listen to as you worship together:

Just as I am by Charlotte Elliot
I will offer up my life by Matt Redman
Ubi caritas by Presses de Taizé
Guide me, O Thou Great Redeemer by William Williams

Read

Bible passages: Ruth 2:8-16, Luke 2:4-7

Ideas to support the readings

This session's reading from Ruth is fairly long. You might like to have a slideshow of illustrations that change while you read. These could be found from a source of free images online and could reflect Boaz's generosity: for example, you could show a welcoming group of women (verse 8) and a jug of water (verse 9) a welcome banner (verses 11-13) some bread or a picnic (verse 14) a bundle of grain (verses 15-16).

* * *

EXPLORE

Reflection

What a relief Boaz's words must have been to Ruth. Chapter 1 verse 7 tells us that she has been on her feet working all morning, and now as the day gets hotter, Boaz has come out to his farm from Bethlehem and spotted her following the workers in his field. Ruth has taken a risk to be there. A new woman, alone in a field full of men who belonged there could have been in grave danger of assault. There could have been competition for the remnants of grain that the poor were allowed to pick up; for someone unfamiliar with the system, there could have been accusations of taking too much or from the wrong place.

Boaz himself could have been hostile, or just indifferent, to this new foreigner taking advantage of the Levitical law to glean some of his harvest for herself. Instead, in verses 8-9 he welcomes her generously. He offers her inclusion in their community, telling her to stick with the other women working for him in the field; he guarantees her safety, telling the young men to leave her alone; he provides for her by letting her know that she is welcome to share the water available to his workers. In verses 14-16, he goes further: he shares their lunch with Ruth, then tells his harvesters to let her take grain even if it hasn't fallen and to pull some out of their bundles and leave it behind deliberately for her to pick up. He wants to make sure that she goes home with plenty. He goes far further than the law demands in his welcome of this foreigner.

When Ruth asks why Boaz is being so generous, it comes to light that he knows who she is. His response in verse 12 is interesting because it focuses on God: Boaz recognises that Ruth has come 'under God's wings' for refuge. He prays that she may have a 'full reward from the LORD' for doing so, but perhaps he also recognises his own part in providing that reward, in representing the God who he knows provides refuge and comfort, and welcomes the outsider in. For Boaz, Ruth deserves refuge not because she has approached him, not even just because of her kindness to Naomi, but because she has approached and trusted God. And Boaz knows that, in this situation, he represents God: as a member of God's people, it is his duty to show God's promised welcome. How often do we remember that we represent Jesus, as members of the body of Christ, in just the same way?

Boaz has a particular reason for believing that God welcomes the outsider: his own mother, Rahab, was a foreigner, who married into Israel after her rescue from Jericho (you can find her story in Joshua, chapters 2 and 6). There was nobody better placed than Boaz to have compassion for Ruth, even before considering that he was related to Naomi's late husband.

A thousand years later in the same town, Mary and Joseph find themselves pushed to the edges. The house is full, the guest room already taken, but there is a bit of space downstairs with the animals. Mary, feeling the first pangs of labour, must have been perplexed. All the joy of her meeting with Elizabeth, her song about the lowly being lifted up, Gabriel's greeting of 'favoured one' must have swum together in her mind as she contemplated this place where the son of God was about to be born.

But Mary had already, nine months earlier, declared herself to be the servant of the Lord (Luke 1:38) and said, 'Let it be with me according to your word'. Although we are not given an insight into her thoughts at this precise moment, that quiet trust is what we know her for: from the moment that she treasures the words of the shepherds, storing them in her heart to consider later, to the moment at the wedding in Cana when she tells the servants to do whatever Jesus tells them, to her silent presence at the foot of the cross. Mary, like Ruth before her, has placed herself entirely under God's wings.

Ruth and Mary both do receive God's gift of protection, of loving communities, husbands, a support network around them; but they both began their journeys of obedience before those things were given or even promised. They had no guarantee of safety, but they placed themselves under God's wings anyway and came to the edge of the field, the edge of the house.

As the Christmas story unfolds, the shepherds run to the manger, and the magi see the star and begin travelling from far-off countries. As Ruth's story unfolds, we see God beginning to shape the ancestry of David, the one who will lead to tiny Bethlehem becoming known as the royal City of David. We see how the edge becomes the centre because God is there with the women who trust him.

Discussion

- In Ruth 2:14, when Boaz gives Ruth some lunch, it says 'she ate until she was satisfied, and she had some left over'. Does that remind you of a phrase from one of the Gospels? (Compare Luke 9:15-17!) How else has Boaz acted in a Jesus-like way so far?
- Who are the people on the edges of our society and community? How can we be more like Boaz in our welcome?
- What does it mean to be a member of the body of Christ? How does it affect the way we deal with other people?
- In ancient Israel, both Mary and Ruth (and Naomi) needed the protection and provision of men to survive. Things are different today, but what do single people in our communities need to thrive - and how can we help provide it?
- Mary and Ruth both obeyed God before any guarantee of the good things that were to come. How do you keep obeying when there is no sign of things getting better? How can their stories give us hope in times of doubt and despair?

Group activity
You will need:

Something to represent a shelter. Depending on the size of your group and the space, this could be anything from a shoebox on its side to the empty stable from the Christmas nativity set, or a space under a table or, if in a church, under a cross or in front of the altar. Alternatively, you could cut out the shape of a pair of wings to reflect Boaz's statement to Ruth about coming under God's wings for refuge.

Some little figures, one for each member of the group. These could be simple paper cut-out people, or little wooden human-shaped pegs (available from Baker Ross and similar craft stores) or pebbles.

Have the 'shelter' set up, and scatter the figures around the room. Ask everyone to move around the room and find a figure to bring back. They could then decorate this to represent themselves; either abstractly, or by making it look like them, or by writing or illustrating something that they feel represents them.

Say: these figures have been scattered and alone. They each have their own individual worries, hopes and dreams. It is so easy to feel alone with a problem. Sometimes we even feel alone with success and joy, if there is nobody to share it with. But we can come to God for refuge. We can place ourselves under God's wings.

Ask everyone to move to the shelter and place their figure there before standing back.

When all the figures are in the shelter, say: when we all move towards God, we also move towards each other. The figures in the shelter are together now: they have made a community within God's refuge, and found others in their place of safety. Here we all are, together. If we are all here because we have come to God for refuge, then we have a responsibility to each other, to make sure that we all find refuge and safety here, as Boaz did for Ruth. This can become the place where Christ is born in our midst, as he was for Mary at the first Christmas. Though we may feel on the edge of things, with God, the edge becomes the centre.

* * *

RESPOND

Pray

To end this session, find a way to pray for people at the margins of your own community and for those who work with them. Depending on your situation, these will be unique to your group. You may want to prepare by asking members of the group for their ideas, as well as researching the areas below.

Find out what organisations and help, if any, exist in your community for:

- The elderly
- The homeless
- Refugees and migrants
- People with learning difficulties
- People with disabilities
- Children in hospital, or who cannot access school

- LGBT people
- You can probably think of others relevant to your specific community.

If you have representatives of these communities in your group, you could ask for their help to gather information.

Use a map of your local community and display it alongside any leaflets, news cuttings or photographs that are relevant to these people groups. Provide post-it notes and pens for people to write or draw their prayers and stick them in the relevant areas. Encourage everyone to pray first for the people they know and care about most, and then to find an area they know little about and take some time to read about it and pray for the people involved.

Ponder

Where God is, the margins become the centre. As Christians, we are the body of Christ, and wherever we are, Christ is in us. This week, set yourself some reminders on your phone, (or on some post-it notes stuck around the house, car and in your wallet!) that God is with you and Christ is in you. When you see the reminder, take a moment to look at your surroundings and imagine Jesus in that place, with you and whoever else you are with. Let the moment become the centre of everything, and watch and listen to see what Jesus will do with it.

Prepare

For leaders: For the next session, you will need a cross and a crib (either a nativity scene or just Jesus in a manger) to set up centrally where everyone can see them. There are also some words to display during the reading and activity, which you could do centrally on a screen or flipchart, or individually on printed sheets. You may want to choose readers in advance to take the parts of Boaz, the other kinsman and Simeon in the readings.

For group members: You might like to read chapter 3 of Ruth, as the next session skips ahead to chapter 4.

Chapter 4

Session Four

Kinsman, Redeemer

BEGIN

Introduction
In our set readings for this session, we have skipped over chapter 3 of Ruth and landed in chapter 4, but if you can, do read both chapters. They tell the story of how Naomi, realising Boaz's relationship to her late husband Elimelech, arranges for Ruth to ask him to 'redeem' her - basically, to inherit her along with Elimelech's property as his next-of-kin.

This is the hardest part of the book of Ruth to tell, because it is so steeped in unfamiliar ancient law and the uncomfortable concept of women as men's property, so offensive to modern ears. However, there are only a few things that we need to understand to guide us through this part of the story.

Boaz, by law, is a possible kinsman-redeemer. Breaking down that term, a kinsman is somebody from the same family; a redeemer is someone with the right or ability to redeem (take back or buy back) and restore. The word 'redeemer' is rightly more familiar to us because of Jesus, and that is not the wrong link to be making here. As Boaz was to Ruth, Jesus is a kinsman to us: he is one of us, fully human. He is also fully God, and in his divinity he has both the right and the ability to redeem: to take us back, to restore us from our lost and fallen state where we were estranged from God. So Jesus performs for humanity the same action that Boaz performs for Ruth.

But there is more going on in Ruth's story. We see wisdom from Naomi, as she works out the connection and teaches Ruth the correct approach; we see obedience from Ruth as she once again puts herself on the line for Naomi; and we see a certain amount of cunning from Boaz, as he deals with the fact that there is a kinsman-redeemer with more right than he has to Elimelech's property, but less interest in Ruth's well-being. In fact, beyond the legalese and local customs, it's quite the nail-biting finish - and we will find that there are just as many echoes of Christ in Ruth's actions as there are in those of Boaz.

We will be skipping ahead in Mary's story, too, to look at her encounter with Simeon, who was able to see and predict Jesus' role as redeemer, not just of Israel, but of the Gentile nations too, echoing back to Ruth's inclusion in Israel and in the bloodline of David. But don't worry, we're not missing the birth of Jesus - there will be two important births in the next session!

Opening question/activity

Have you ever lost anything precious and found it again? What did you have to do to get it back? Share the story with the people around you.

WORSHIP

Pray

Jesus our brother, today we are thinking about what you came into our world to do, and everything that it cost you. Thank you for your great, redeeming love for us. As we read and talk together, may we learn how to show others a little of your generous, welcoming, sacrificial love, in your name. Amen.

Sing

Here are some suggestions for hymns and songs which you could sing or listen to as you worship together:
Reckless Love by Cory Asbury
How He Loves by John Mark McMillan
Servant King by Graham Kendrick
When I Survey by Isaac Watts

Read

Bible passages: Ruth 4:1-12, Luke 2:25-35

Ideas to support the readings

If possible, while everyone listens to the passages being read, display the following words somewhere and ask people to try to spot them coming up in the passages. We will return to look at these words in the group activity.
CONSOLATION, REDEEM, INHERIT, NAME, PRESENCE, CUSTOM.

Once again, it may help to make the reading clearer if they are read in parts. For the reading from Ruth, give parts to Boaz and the other next-of-kin, and ask everyone to read verses 11-12 in chorus when the witnesses speak. In the reading from Luke, ask someone to read the part of Simeon.

EXPLORE

Reflection
Each of our passages today has a flavour of custom and the law. The scene in Ruth takes place at the gate of the city, where business, social and legal transactions were settled in the presence of witnesses. There, Boaz confronts the man with a closer right to redeem Naomi's husband's property, and acquires it from him.

In Luke, the scene takes place at the temple in Jerusalem, where Mary and Joseph go to follow the law and make a sacrifice for purification after the birth of a child. The custom is in remembrance of the Passover, when God freed the Hebrew people from the Egyptians with the death of the Egyptians' first-born sons. Since that point, first-born sons were considered to belong to God (Exodus 12; Numbers 3:13) and in the ritual, the parents acknowledge this and 'redeem' the son with a sacrifice.

Boaz seems to use a bit of cunning in his approach to the other kinsman of Elimelech. He mentions that Naomi is selling a field first, and the man seems eager to exercise his right to redeem it. Then Boaz adds, almost as an afterthought, that the field comes with a wife whose son will inherit the property to continue the name of their dead relative. This is much more of a problem: it means that the man would have to give up his own name and inheritance rights to pass them to Ruth's children. He refuses and leaves Boaz free to redeem the property.

Having this conversation in front of witnesses and according to custom shows that Boaz is being completely open and fair; his claim to the property now cannot be contested. It also shows how the sacrifice that Boaz himself is making is one that others would not be prepared to make. Redemption always comes at a cost. For Boaz, it is not just the cost of the field, but his own prospects of marriage, name and inheritance in exchange for continuing Elimelech's name.

When we think of Jesus' redemption of the world, we think of the cost of the cross and of his suffering. A passage in Philippians considers other costs:

'...though he was in the form of God,
did not regard equality with God as something to be exploited,
but emptied himself,
taking the form of a slave,
being born in human likeness.' (Philippians 2:6-7)

This emptying of self is what we see in the incarnation, when we think about the small, fragile infant Jesus, vulnerable in our world even though he was God. That is the infant Simeon recognises as the Messiah when Mary and Joseph bring him to the temple. Simeon had been promised by God that he would not die before seeing the Messiah; when he sets eyes on Jesus, he recognises that this promise has been fulfilled. In that moment, full of the Holy Spirit, perhaps Simeon sees that the baby in his arms has given everything up to be there with him.

Boaz is not the only one who reflects something of that aspect of Christ's character. Even more reminiscent of it is Ruth, who left her home and came empty-handed to a new country. Her story looks forward to Jesus leaving his heavenly home and emptying himself to be with us on earth. Like Jesus, Ruth was vulnerable, putting herself at risk for the sake of Naomi, first by going to work in the field and then by offering herself to the mercy of Boaz at the threshing floor. Just as Ruth did it because she loved Naomi, and wanted to help and rescue her, so Jesus did it for the love of humanity, wanting to help and rescue us; and both those sacrifices ended in redemption.

The witnesses at the gate name some of the great women of Israel, thus welcoming Ruth, a Gentile (non-Jew), into the nation. They wish that she will 'bestow a name in Bethlehem,' a prayer that is certainly answered beyond what any of them could imagine.

Back in the reading from Luke, Simeon stands in the temple, holding the infant Jesus in his arms, and calls him 'a light for revelation to the Gentiles and for glory to your people Israel.' He prophetically imagines Jesus opening the kingdom of God beyond Israel to the Gentile nations, at last opening the door to everyone who, like Ruth, knows that they can seek refuge in the God of Israel.

Most of us reading this today are Gentiles who have now been included in that promise. Jesus' emptying of himself, his sacrifice to redeem us, has included us with him as children of God. He has given us his name, and along with him, we will inherit the kingdom of God. The door is open for us. That is the vision Simeon had as he held the vulnerable baby in his arms. That is the good news of Christmas.

Discussion

- What is the furthest you have ever travelled to see someone special? Who was it?

- Imagine that you were in the crowd of witnesses at the gate (in the reading from Ruth) or in the temple (in the reading from Luke). What did you see and hear? How do you feel about what you have witnessed?
- Have you ever witnessed an act of mercy, rescue or redemption, however small? What happened?
- How would you express the good news of Christmas in your own words?

Group activity
Provide a list of the following words, either centrally (eg on a PowerPoint) or individually on a printout:
CONSOLATION, REDEEM, INHERIT, NAME, PRESENCE, CUSTOM.

In small groups or pairs, ask everyone to choose one or two of those words and find them in the Bible readings. Many of them occur in some form in both readings: if the exact word doesn't occur, a different form of it might (eg redeem/redemption).

Pause and compare notes.

Then ask the groups to create a mind map of their word, by writing it centrally on a piece of paper and writing or drawing any connections with the word around the outside. These could be where the word appears elsewhere in the Bible, what it has to do with Christmas or the Gospel, what it means to the personal experiences of the people in the groups, or quotes from prose or poetry - anything at all.

Display the sheets and have some time for everyone to move

around and look at them, exploring and talking about the links that have been made.

* * *

RESPOND

Pray

Set up a plain cross, or a depiction of the crucifixion, where everyone can see it. Next to it, set up a crib scene or just a baby in a manger.

Read Philippians 2:5-8 out loud. Invite everyone to think about the words, and to thank Jesus silently in their own way, while some quiet music plays. (You could use one of the suggestions from the 'Sing' heading above, or try 'Once Again' by Matt Redman, which takes its lyrics from this passage in Philippians.)

At the end of the song, read Philippians 2:9-11 out loud, or if possible, invite everyone to read that passage together, and say 'Amen' at the end.

Ponder

During this week as we approach Christmas (or on Christmas day itself, if that happens before the final session) try to find a few peaceful moments to read Philippians 2:5-11 again, by your own crib or tree, and remind yourself of the wonder of the incarnation.

Prepare

For leaders: For the next session, you may want to provide festive food and decorations for a celebratory atmosphere! For the readings, you will need print-outs for the group (or a

powerpoint display) with the parts to say together highlighted.
For the activity, you may want to provide blank Christmas cards and/or art supplies.
For group members: Before the next session, you might like to look at the readings and find the parts that will be read in chorus.

Chapter 5

Session Five

Born in Bethlehem

BEGIN

Introduction
Happy Christmas! This is the Christmas session, so it is shorter and more celebratory. You may be having it just before Christmas, or in the days and weeks afterwards (remember, it's still Christmas for twelve days after the 25th!) It's a chance to celebrate together as a group, finish both the Bible stories and share what has been learned across the Advent sessions.

In the Bible readings for this session, two babies are born in Bethlehem. Although they are born a thousand years apart, they are members of the same lineage. Ruth's son Obed was the father of Jesse, the father of King David, who gave Bethlehem its title of 'Royal David's city' as we sing today; Jesus was born there to show his descent from David, as prophesied in Isaiah 11 verses 1 and 10, Micah 5:2, and many other passages of the

Old Testament. In this session, we will look at the similarities between these two special births.

Opening activity
Gather together over some festive food!

* * *

WORSHIP

Pray
Father, as we gather together to celebrate, we praise you for the birth of your beloved son Jesus, and we thank you that you loved the world so much that you sent him so that everyone who believes in him might have everlasting life. As we learn about two Bethlehem births, may we grow in understanding of what Jesus' birth meant for the world and for each of us. Amen.

Sing
At last, it's time for Christmas carols! Ask the group to choose some of their favourites - but make sure that at least one verse of 'Once in Royal David's City' is included!

Read
Bible passages: Ruth 4:13-17; Luke 2:8-20

Ideas to support the readings
These readings both involve a chorus of voices, so prompt everyone beforehand and read those parts together as a group! (You may wish to hand out the readings with those parts highlighted.) In the reading from Ruth, it's the voices of the

women (verses 14-15 and 17); in the Luke passage, it's the voices of the angels (verse 14) and the shepherds (verse 15).

* * *

EXPLORE

Reflection

Perhaps the most important line in this ending of the story of Ruth is in Ruth 4:14, when the women bless the Lord for providing her with a next-of-kin. The story does not only end happily for Ruth, with a wedding and a baby; but due to Ruth's obedience, Naomi's wisdom and Boaz's careful legal wranglings, this baby will now continue Naomi and Elimelech's family line, and will inherit their property. It is harder to see with modern eyes, but Ruth has managed to restore Naomi's loss and social status by providing her with a next-in-line for Naomi's dead husband and sons. That is why, in verse 17, the women say that a son has been born to Naomi, rather than to Ruth, and call Obed 'a restorer of life' (verse 15).

Naomi, who had lost her family, has been drawn back into that family. Ruth, who left her people, has been given a new people. And in that line in verse 14, also easily missed unless you look at the footnotes of the translation, is the fact that the words used for 'next-of-kin' are the same as the ones that have been used to describe Boaz all along: 'the one with the right to redeem'.

Baby Obed, then, is a tiny redeemer for Naomi and Ruth; but for Christians reading this story today, the way he continues that family line is even more important. The father of Jesse and grandfather of King David, he is the 27th great-grandfather of

Jesus, whose Bethlehem birth we are celebrating. (Incidentally, this is how we know that Boaz was the son of Rahab: in the genealogy in the first chapter of Matthew, they are both mentioned along with Ruth and Obed, in verse 5.) In the famous message of the angel to the shepherds in Luke 2:10-12, Bethlehem is only called the City of David because Ruth gave birth to Obed there a thousand years earlier.

The story of Ruth is a wonderful gift from God. Hidden away in the genealogy of Jesus, against the background of evil and violence in the chaotic book of Judges, these pictures of mercy and redemption - Ruth leaving her home to redeem Naomi, Boaz putting aside his inheritance to redeem Ruth - foreshadow the arrival of God into our world, leaving his heavenly glory to become one of us, allowing us alongside him to become inheritors of his kingdom.

That's the wonder of the story we saw unfold in our reading from Luke, as heaven touched earth in the song of the angels, praising God and proclaiming peace: peace against the chaotic background, peace amid the world's warring, peace between earth and heaven because of a baby born into a small, ordinary, obedient, God-loving family in the little town of Bethlehem.

Discussion

- What pictures of salvation do you see in the book of Ruth? How are Boaz and Ruth like Jesus in their actions?
- What, for you, is the significance of the book of Ruth taking place alongside the book of Judges? How can this offer hope today?

- Can you think of other examples in the Bible of God's plans taking place among small families and ordinary people, rather than kings and leaders?
- What is the significance of Jesus being born where he was?
- Has anything from this Advent course changed the way you will think about and celebrate Christmas this year?

Group activity

The angels explained to the shepherds why the birth of Jesus was good news; the Bethlehem women told Naomi how Obed would make a difference to her life. Looking back at their words and adding your own, write a Christmas card for a friend or neighbour explaining why the Christmas story is good news and how it can change a person's life.

Alternatively, work together as a group (or in small groups) to make banners or artwork to display around the church or put onto social media, explaining and celebrating the good news of the birth of Jesus Christ.

* * *

RESPOND

Pray

Jesus, we thank you for the story of Ruth. Thank you that it's told in the Bible so that we can read it today. Thank you for the way it weaves in and out of your own story, for Ruth's obedience in becoming part of your family, and for Ruth's sacrifice and journey which reminds us of your sacrifice for us.

Thank you for showing us that ordinary lives and loving duties are important in your story and great in your eyes. Whatever is happening in the world around us, help us to keep our eyes on you and to look out for you working in the everyday, this Christmas and always. Amen.

Ponder

What do you hope you will still remember from this course next year?

About the Author

Amy Scott Robinson is the author of five Advent-themed books including this one, as well as other resources, devotionals and children's books. She also writes as a contributor to Engage Worship and the Church Times. After studying English at Christ's College, Cambridge, she trained as a teacher and began writing for a charity providing school assemblies, before becoming a performance storyteller herself. She loves hanging around medieval churches, reading fairy tales and playing with puppets. She lives in Bury St Edmunds where she is married to the vicar of St Mary's.

They Sang

ISBN: 9781838581121 Product code: 1501692

Have you ever wished the world was more like a musical, with characters bursting into song at the slightest provocation?
In the nativity story, there are four sudden, Spirit-filled songs from the heart, and they're all still used in the rhythm of liturgy: Zechariah's song (the Benedictus) Mary's song (Magnificat) the song of the angels (Gloria in Excelsis) and Simeon's song (Nunc Dimittis).
In 'They Sang', Amy Scott Robinson uses four Advent studies to guide small groups to explore these ancient poems of praise and prophecy, and a fifth invites you to discover your own song.

Sleigh Bells & Stables

ISBN: 9781838581770 Product code: 1501732

Packed full of seasonal stories, poems and suggestions for the church family to share during Advent and Christmas, this book will become your go-to resource for everything from crib services to Christmas fairs.
Whether you're looking for a school assembly on the theme of Advent, a reading for a carol service or an idea to invite the whole community into a new festive tradition, you will find it in this compilation that covers every occasion from Advent through to Candlemas.